Well I'm Blowed

Notes from the Brass Band

Ian W Wright

i2f Publishing
6 Burton Close
Wheathampstead
Herts AL4 8LU
Tel: +44 (0) 1438 833730

Web: www.i2fpublishing.com

First published 2012 © i2f Publishing

The right of Ian W. Wright to be identified as the author of this work has been asserted by him in accordance with the Copyright, Designs and Patents Act of 1998.

ISBN 978-0-9563617-8-3

A catalogue record for this publication is registered with the British Library.

All images used in this book are sourced from: http://commons.wikimedia.org and are thought to be in the public domain and free from any copywrite restrictions.

All rights reserved. No part of this publication may be reproduced, stored in a retrieval system, or transmitted in any form or by any means, electronic, mechanical, photocopying, recording, or otherwise without either the prior written permission of the publishers or a licence permitting restricted copying in the united Kingdom issued by the Copyright Licensing Agency Ltd, Saffron House, 6-10 Kirby Street, London EC1N 8TS. This book may not be lent, resold, hired out or otherwise disposed of by way of trade in any form of binding or cover than that in which it is published without prior consent of the publishers.

Contents

Foreword	4
Winds of Change	6
The Carnival	12
Steaming Along	17
Getting the Bird	35
Playing for the Queen	40
Grave Consequences	44
The Band Ghost	50
The Seeing Eye	57
Economic Living	63
Christmas Carolling	68
Epilogue	75
About the Author	76

Foreword

All around the world there is nothing which so fires the imagination and enthusiasm as a good parade. For the British, the pomp and pageantry of a Royal event guarantees television's highest viewing figures. Whilst not everyone can become intimately involved in such grand events, the childhood dream of most to march at the head of a grand parade is within reach through the brass band movement.

The involvement of youngsters in any form of band or musical group is to be strongly recommended as through this medium they will develop confidence, social skills and a team spirit which will be of great assistance as they pass into the adult world of work.

Playing in a band is infectious; players who leave to have families or because of work commitments almost always return to a band eventually - it gets into the blood and there is seldom a time when bandsmen get together which doesn't generate an amusing incident or anecdote.

The events in this book are centred around a fictitious band and use fictitious characters - however, the author has been associated with various brass bands over many years and this collection of anecdotes is based upon his experiences.

Each tale in this book is based upon actual events or characters, only the names, locations and certain details have been changed to protect the guilty. This was considered desirable in view of the sensitive nature of some of the events.

Winds of Change

The nineteenth century saw great changes in the English pattern of life. Not since the Romans invaded to enforce their ideas of civilisation and the subsequent Saxon settlement with its burning and pillaging and feudal system had change been so rapid.

In the nineteenth century, industry developed in the towns and cities and then rapidly overflowed to the surrounding villages and countryside, changing as it went the whole appearance of the landscape and way of life of the resident population. Every river and stream became the focus of factories large and small with tall chimneys to take the choking smoke above the immediate residents but distributing it over wide areas and polluting the previously clean and fertile land.

New dams were built to capture the water for these factories so denying it to the farmers and livestock lower down the valleys until it had been well polluted with the dirt and effluent of the crude industrial processes. Housing developments sprang up around the factories taking up valuable land and ensuring that the locals, who had been used to self sufficiency, no longer had enough land within easy reach to grow their vegetables or keep their pigs and had therefore to either move away or become dependent upon the factory owned shops which blossomed and flourished. This then was the "civilisation" of rural England which achieved by stealth what no previous forcible efforts had been capable of.

Against this background of oppression and depression, however, there came one shining ray of sunshine, one expression of the suppressed joy and hope of the population, one joining together in a cloaked spirit of united rebellion. What was this miracle sent to bring joy and happiness to city and countryside alike? - it was the Brass Band. Founded out of poverty and exploitation the brass band movement spread rapidly throughout the country as workers from every facet of life found that they could meet together and join in a common pleasure which was actually encouraged and often financed by the factory and mill owners.

But why did brass bands become so popular so quickly? The reasons were various, who could fail to be stirred by the beautiful melodies or by the stirring marches and the depth of sound produced by the bass section, who could resist marching or dancing happily alongside a parade led by a band? The band gave expression to the pent up emotions of the workforce and called up visions of free and happy times - and yet, this music could be made by all.

The clever design of the instruments meant that with very little tuition a beginner could join in with the rest of the band within a matter of weeks and feel he was making a worthwhile contribution and, as all the instruments were of similar design, he could move around the band from instrument to instrument using the same basic techniques and fingering of the valves, until he found the instrument which suited him best.

It wasn't long, of course, before the potential of brass bands was recognised by the influential institutions of the day, particularly the Salvation Army who embraced the idea whole-heartedly and founded their own bands in every town and city, playing in the streets to help swell the membership and funds of their cause. To this day some of the best players in the brass band movement start their training in their local Salvation Army band.

The advertising potential of such a popular movement was also not lost upon the employers. Many of the larger factories established bands bearing their own name and from this came the well known bands of Black Dyke Mills, Grimethorpe Colliery, Hammond's Sauce works and countless more.

Mankind being what it is, it wasn't possible for such an idyllic movement to survive for long without a spirit of competition creeping in and soon the various commercial bands were holding contests to try to outperform the bands of their business competitors. This, of course, developed until national competitions were being organised and some bands began to devote much of their efforts into entering or preparing for competitions.

Into this highly charged atmosphere was born the Brassford Silver Prize Band. Founded at the height of this enthusiasm in 1870, the band began life as a mediocre collection of misfits and dropouts who, to while away long winter evenings, began to meet each Wednesday night in the Village Hall to be cajoled by George Parker, the landlord of the Fox and Duck, into producing half recognisable melodies from the motley collection of instruments they had managed to assemble.

The only new instrument belonged to Harold Brown. This was a shining silver cornet by one of the best makers which he had bought with a legacy from a long forgotten aunt. Because of the status this instrument gave him, he was the obvious choice for Principal Cornet. The fact that he had not yet mastered the notes was of little relevance as all the band agreed that, so long as Harry was going to blow his discords with such gusto, he may as well do so from the front and display his instrumental finery to the band's advantage.

Such down to earth common sense has always been a feature of bandsmen. It also, to them, seemed common sense to allow the owner of the local public house to be their conductor as it has always been essential for a band to have a suitable refuge at which to refuel after a hard rehearsal.

Gradually the standard of the band improved and with it it's standing in the local community, achieving, at the same time, a degree of respectability almost on a par with the local church whose sponsorship and tolerance was relied upon to a great extent for public performances. The original bands were largely male dominated but were encouraged by the womenfolk. As some wives were heard to mutter, *"at least when they are at band rehearsals you know where they are"* - the whole village knew! During these early days practising was, for some, as much of a problem as we find today in our present cramped society.

The pressures of space were not so acute but the relentless pursuit of perfection was often something of a trial to other members of the family. One notable case was Huw Jones of Dale Head Farm. You would think that having originated in the musical environment of mid-Wales, his family would have appreciated his efforts but, on the contrary, his wife would have none of it and he was banished from the house with his euphonium. He fortunately had a large barn about two fields away which he used as a cow shed and often the strained tones of 'Myffanwy' could be heard drifting across the dale from this direction. He swore to the end that his music made the cows give more milk.

The village of Brassford sits in a beautiful sleepy valley in North Derbyshire just on the fringes of the steel making areas of South Yorkshire. Its local industries fortunately did not severely affect the landscape and the remaining mill buildings are small and now blend in with their surroundings. Many have gone altogether as the industrial revolution lost momentum and began to focus on larger factories in the nearby cities.

Many of the villagers now commute daily into these cities or work away from the area altogether, only returning at weekends and for holidays. So the pace of village life has once again slowed and, apart from its larger size, the village is now much as it was before civilisation marched past. Still going strong, however, is the Brassford Silver Prize Band. No one can now remember where the term 'Silver Prize Band' came from, certainly no silver prize now exists but, just in case one ever turns up again, the name stays and lends to the band that certain class and degree of professionalism which looks so important on the hand-written notices of forthcoming concerts displayed outside the local church hall.

Band members are now of all ages and of both sexes and come from a wide area, some from the city and others from surrounding villages up to twenty miles away. The spirit of the band is strong and its members are like an extended family. For many, the regular weekly rehearsal is an event anticipated with the utmost pleasure.

The Carnival

Still the highlight of Brassford band's year is the village carnival when they lead a parade through the village to the field just on the outskirts in which the main events are held. There is seldom a year goes by without this parade producing some source of amusement to last the participants through the year. The occurrence of a couple of years ago is typical. One of the longer serving members is the local postmistress, Janet Long.

She has been playing the tenor horn in the band for as long as anyone can remember and must be well into her seventies, yet she turns up for every event whatever the weather. This particular year was to be her downfall in more ways than one. It was a warm July day, the streets were resplendent with bunting and garlands and the local population had been reinforced by a copious supply of townspeople lining the narrow streets and jostling for the best positions.

Local people hung out of every window anxious not to miss a minute of this once-a-year event and straining to see their friends and relatives taking part in the procession. The band, resplendent in their red and black uniforms, led the procession buoyed up by the cheers of the crowd. Immediately behind, the carnival queen looked radiant riding reclined upon the bonnet of her car decorated with hundreds of tissue paper flowers and flanked on each side by her maids-in-waiting.

As the parade wound its way up the main street between the crowds of excited children and their parents a wisp of pink fabric began to make an appearance below the hem of Janet's black skirt.

This may not have been so noticeable had her legs not also been clad in the black woollen stockings which she habitually wore. The crowd's eyes were instantly drawn to this dramatic pink line which, as the band marched on, slowly grew until it blossomed into a pair of the largest billowing pink bloomers ever seen. These descended gracefully to Janet's ankles where, with hardly a hesitation she stepped out of them and carried on marching. All this time the look on her face had never changed from her deadpan 'concentrating' face and her step had never faltered except to perhaps shorten just a little as the copious lingerie reached her lower leg.

Of course, half the band were unaware of what was happening behind them and it wasn't until they broke up in the carnival field that the story could be properly circulated. The hilarity was tremendous but Janet took it all in her stride even adding to some of the anecdotes and suggesting that the organisers of the

carnival be prevailed upon to hold it on a less draughty
day the next year. The usual band de-briefing after the
carnival took on a whole new complexion that year.

That wasn't the end of the incident however, for
the following day the bloomers were spotted flying
gustily from the church weathercock adorned with
the words '"Long" drawers' in black letters.

Fortunately, the wind rose during the day
and they were wrenched from their perch
before evening never to be seen again.

That same year, the band had been asked to play
for a while during the carnival and so set up in a
corner of the field not too far from the refreshment
tent. After playing a fine selection of marches
and modern numbers to a largely disinterested
crowd it was decided that a break was in order.

The largest part of the crowd were at the other end
of the field watching the judging of the 'wet T-shirt'
competition, so access to refreshments would not be
hampered. The instruments were put away in their cases
and the music folders closed and the band adjourned to
the beer tent to join the inevitable group of older locals.

The story of Janet's drawers was being reiterated
with 'tasteful' embellishments for the umpteenth time
together with comparative analyses of the various
beers and crisps when a tremendous hullabaloo
erupted outside the tent. Rushing outside, the band
were just in time to see their music, stands and chairs
being scattered and shredded by a prize heifer on

the loose from the show ring. It was being pursued in a half hearted fashion by a couple of young farm hands who seemed at a loss as to how to curtail its exuberant destructiveness so, in the usual spirit of helpfulness, the whole of the band gave chase.

Only after a further complete circuit of the field and ploughing through the wet T-shirt crowds, was the terrified animal eventually cornered close to the show ring from which it had escaped. There then followed a period of mayhem as stall holders and exhibitors tried to restore some semblance of order during which the band decided that it had had quite enough excitement for one year and packed up.

The following year, the band were lucky to survive as far as the carnival field. It had been decided by the carnival committee that the parade would, that year, be led by the local fire engine. The theory was that, if a call came through whilst being on display to the public, it could rush off from the parade without disturbing the proceedings and render its public service.

The engine, however, was rather aged and it is doubtful if it could really go faster than the parade anyway. It was often jokingly blamed by those at the back of the parade for holding them up and causing bunching. This particular year the engine was worse than usual and was obviously in some mechanical distress. The whole of the band, following directly behind it, were completely enveloped in a grey/blue fog of exhaust fumes which made the eyes water and poisoned the lungs.

Most of the route through the village is slightly uphill and playing became more and more impossible. Seeking to ease the situation, instructions were given to fall back and allow the fire engine to go on ahead but our ever vigilant fire crew obviously noticed this and conscientiously reduced their speed to keep the procession together.

With great good luck a fire call did come, for the first time within memory, and the engine peeled off half way up the hill, but there was no more playing that day.

Steaming Along

The eastern sky glowed with a golden fire as Percy Jackson dressed in the front window of his hillside cottage. He threw wide his windows and drew in a deep breath of the fragrant fresh air, heavy with the scent of ripening corn and wild flowers. Looking out over the fields his eye was first drawn to the new line of molehills which had appeared overnight. They ran almost dead straight from his front wall to the crest of a small rise some two hundred yards away and stood out starkly brown against the silvery green of dew laden cobwebbed grass.

Close to the top of the hill a cow was nuzzling at one of the mounds as if puzzled by their cause. In the distance the church clock struck six. Today was going to be a good day!

Finishing dressing, Percy went downstairs and made breakfast. He had been a widower for almost ten years and now lived alone in his small cottage about a mile outside Brassford. Alone, that is, apart from the two dogs who were now anxiously fussing round his legs lest he should forget their morning snack. Both dogs were getting on in years. They had been sheep dogs on local farms but had, for one reason or another, outgrown their usefulness. Bess, the older of the two, had been a champion when she was younger but had met with an accident which had left her with a decided limp and a tendency towards arthritis in the winter. The younger dog, Bob, had started off well but had never calmed down from his puppy like exuberance.

This disquieted the sheep and the harder he tried to master them, the more wild they became. The farmer had persevered for quite some time to train him and steady him down but had finally admitted defeat and had passed him over to Percy as a house dog just after Percy's wife had died. Even age had not dulled Bob's energy and he now beat a tattoo with his tail on the cupboard door as he wagged all his back end in anticipation. Percy gave in and fed the dogs a small bowl of meal while he drank from a steaming pint mug of tea. Sausages and bacon sizzled in the pan as he finished reading last night's paper. He always saved the middle articles of the paper for the next morning as he was always up well before any of the local paper boys.

Finishing his breakfast and piling his crockery into the small stone sink, he pulled on his old boots and set off with his dogs across the moor. He only had to walk about a quarter of a mile up the hill to be in bracken and heather which cracked under his feet releasing the heady smell of honey.

The dogs ran on ahead, heads down, bulldozing their way through the intertwined stems, only occasionally raising them to sniff the wind and make sure that Percy was still in sight. As he reached the crest of the hill, the valley opened up before him and he looked down on Brassford as he had every morning for the last thirty-seven years since moving into the cottage on his wedding day.

This morning there was unusual activity in the village. Even Percy, used to the early rising of a country life, was surprised to see so much happening this early. But this was a special day for the village and the whole valley. Exactly one hundred years ago the railway had arrived and this was the centenary day of the first passenger train to run between Brassford and Castledale at the head of the valley. On that day in 1894, Brassford Band had been given the honour of playing at the new Brassford Halt as the line was dedicated and then accompanying the directors on the first journey to Castledale, playing for them en route.

Bands from the other villages along the way had been involved also, playing on their respective platforms as the train steamed slowly past, but Brassford's honour had been the greatest and they were all given a commemorative medal at the end of the ride much to the disgust of some of their more competitive rivals. Now, one hundred years later, history was to repeat itself and Brassford Band had been invited, no, commanded, to help re-create as closely as possible those original events.

Down in the village the streets were festooned with bunting and garlands of flowers. The station platform was awash with geraniums, chrysanthemums and pelargoniums.

Flags and bunting were everywhere and Percy could see a white line appearing as the edging stones of the platform were whitewashed. A gaily coloured awning was being erected against the small waiting room for it's use as a refreshment hall after the ceremonies. Not for many years had so much activity been seen on this quiet line. These days only local hikers' trains ran up and down the valley and then only in the summer. Regular services had ceased over twenty years ago during the cuts which had severed the links of many country hamlets with the big towns.

However, today the station was bustling and Percy easily recognised the portly figure and shambling gait of George White, its last Station-master, once again attired in his splendid, if somewhat antiquated, uniform. Also to be seen were seven or eight people clad in porters uniforms roughly in the style of the turn of the century. These he assumed to be the railway enthusiasts who had joined with the County Council to stage the event and who had been instrumental over the years in keeping the line open.

As he sat on the low rock which had formed his regular seat for so many years, Percy's mind took him back to the days when he too had been a porter on that same station. He had started there straight from school at fifteen and had worked on the station until it had become just another unmanned 'bus stop' for diesel rail-cars and redundancy had ended his families involvement with the line.

His father had been an engine driver on the line and would often pass through the station on his way over the Pennines. If he was due at around lunch time, Percy's mother would send down a fresh flask of soup for Percy to give him as they paused for water or to take on sheep or cattle for market in Manchester. Old Mr. Jackson had retired a few months before the station closed but Percy had received his notice out of the blue and had been quite indignant for some years. Time, however, had eased the pain and he now looked back on his time there with some fondness. He had always liked the old steam trains and had often gone up to York museum just to be with them. Now, today, he was going to ride on one again and be the centre of attention at the same time.

After sitting for some time, letting the dogs wander and forage in the heather and between the rocks, he pulled himself up against his stick and set off home. The ceremony was to be at twelve o'clock sharp and he had several jobs to do in the house before then. For one thing his uniform trousers needed pressing and his jacket would have to be brushed down to remove the dog hairs which seemed to get everywhere these days.

First of all though, he must service his instrument. This was no easy task as he played the largest instrument in the band, a 'double B flat bass'. It only normally got cleaned just before important events as to do so could take quite some time and effort and used almost a whole tin of silver polish.

The first thing was to strip it down and the four valves were carefully taken from their housings and placed in a plastic wash-bowl with warm soapy water. These were followed by the seven tuning slides, each slightly different in size and shape which made their replacement in the right places easy. Then he took the main part of the instrument outside.

He had found that, to wash out the inside of the pipework, it was easiest to prop the instrument against a fork in the jasmine bush which grew by his garden shed and fill it with soapy water from buckets. This was quite a laborious process requiring several pans of water to be heating on the Calor gas cooker at the same time as he attacked the inner contortions of the tubes with a long bottle brush.

After about half an hour and no small amount of bad language as the Bass had toppled over and drenched his feet, Percy was satisfied with that part and turned his attention to the smaller parts. These were again bottle brushed, rinsed, wiped down and left to dry on the draining board. Now came the hard work. It never ceased to surprise Percy just how much surface area of shiny metal could be compressed into such a small space. The more metal he polished, the more there seemed to be and most of it seemed to be hidden away in difficult corners which required ingenuity to reach with the polishing cloth.

But he would not skimp the job, he never skimped a job, that had been his one failing in life for he could not bear to leave anything he tackled until he had achieved what he perceived as perfection and thus was often late for other things. It took over an hour to polish the instrument and the tuning slides and only then did Percy allow himself a sit down and a glass of his home made beer.

As he sat drinking it, he greased the tuning slides and refitted them, being careful to avoid getting greasy finger-mark on the newly polished metal, and oiled and reassembled the valves, checking that each was in its correct position and was seated properly before screwing home its cap. Noting with some disdain that much of the grease had transferred itself to his glass, he wiped it off with the rag on which he had cleaned his hands, drained it down and set to testing the instrument. The deep bass notes rolled back from the hill and after playing a few scales Percy put down his instrument and sat back with a satisfied grin. Now it was time for the ironing.

Electricity had not yet reached Percy's cottage or, at least, it could have done had he been inclined to pay the cost of installing a wire across the fields from Russett Farm, but having lived all his life without that luxury, he didn't see the need and so he put his two old flat irons on the gas rings and turned his attention to the table. Not finding the need for an ironing board either, he turned back the oilcloth covering of the kitchen table revealing a thick brown protective felt underneath and simply covered this with a worn cotton sheet.

One of the irons was beginning to 'sing' which told him instinctively that it was ready and so, spitting on it's sole and receiving a reassuring hiss in reply, he laid into the black serge trousers with gusto. When he had finished, his whole uniform looked brand new. He had re ironed his white shirt, starching the collar and cuffs so that they now shone like polished plastic, the creases in the front of his trouser legs looked as if they would cut anything they touched and he had pressed his jacket so that there was not a crease on it.

Brushing the crown of his uniform cap and fixing his gold and silver epaulets back on to his jacket he now declared himself ready to meet his public.

The band began to assemble at about 10:45 a.m. in the car park at the far end of the village. Before the main ceremony at the station there was to be a grand parade through the village to escort the High Sheriff of the County and other local dignitaries to the station.

By eleven o'clock quite a crowd had formed. There were several floats on lorries and carts pulled by tractors all decorated with multicoloured flowers and carrying pretty girls from all the surrounding area. It was just like the May Queen Carnivals except that most of the floats had a railway theme. The largest had the coat of arms of the old Midland Railway Company standing about ten feet high on each side, made of mud filled frames covered with appropriate coloured flower petals, and the cab of the lorry was made to look like the front of a steam locomotive complete with tall chimney dressed in black crepe.

Another float, pulled behind a tractor, was a faithful replica of the first station building which had been built on the back of a large hay-cart in wood and then covered all over in flowers and lichens. The colours of these flowers had been very carefully chosen and intermixed so that, from a little distance, the building looked real and appeared to have the grey rough stone walls so characteristic of the area and the usual browner sandstone roofing stones.

The windows and doors were depicted in geranium and rose petals of a dark red which matched the famous Midland red exactly. Even the curtains to the windows and the hanging baskets outside the doors were exactly as depicted on the original painting hanging in the County Library from which the design had been taken.

Between the floats were people in fancy dress and a group in giant costumes of a train driver and fireman, the Station Master and a porter all in the dress of a hundred years ago. The civic delegation arrived at ten past eleven in two open backed Rolls Royce tourers of the 1920's and took their place in the centre of the procession. Just as the church clock struck 11:15 the band launched into the first march and the procession set off.

The large float led the way just behind a police motor cyclist with the band coming next. Then came a float with large boards on each side showing a map of the railway line through the valley picked out in flowers on a mossy background. The villages and higher hills were shown pictorially in bark or seeds and name labels indicated all the important places.

Following this were the giant figures and the other floats intermingled with groups of the local school children who had been doing projects on the anniversary and had made suitable banners which they carried along proudly.

The procession passed slowly down Main Street amid crowds of cheering people. It seemed that the whole of Derbyshire had turned out for the event and, as the parade made its way towards the station, all the onlookers joined on behind or scuttled through the side alleyways to watch the spectacle again as it reached its destination. By the time the station hove into view, the extra police drafted in from all the outlying communities were having trouble maintaining a clear path for the procession to pass. There were so many people. All along the way the streets and adjoining buildings were decked with flowers, bunting and garlands and now the station approach was surmounted at frequent intervals by arches of flowers right across the road.

The station itself was a picture. Gone was the dismal air of an unmanned rural station which had pervaded the dilapidated buildings and abandoned ticket kiosk for over twenty years and in its place had returned the bright friendliness which had once made it a place for the community to be proud of. The buildings had been scoured of graffiti and given a new coat of paint - Midland red of course - and the grimy, stone flagged platforms had been steam cleaned and brushed until they appeared freshly quarried.

The platform edges sported a coat of pristine white paint and every wall seemed to be home to troughs of brilliant flowers. It was a truly amazing transformation. A large stage edged with floral baskets had been set up over one of the two lines with a dais facing the platform on which the public were now jostling for places.

Adjacent to the dais were chairs for the band to the left and for the civic and other dignitaries to the right.
The band were to play a couple of numbers to set the mood before the speeches began and struck up with the march Belphegor which had been played at the original opening ceremony of the line which they followed with an arrangement of Coronation Scot, the well known radio tune.

Then started the speeches, the first by the local area controller of British Rail who declared his delight that such a beautiful line still existed in such wonderful condition; presumably he believed its present decorous state to be the norm and wished to take all credit for it. This obviously began to irritate some of the local enthusiasts who had given up a great deal of spare time to achieve the transformation. The events in the station were being relayed to the throng outside the station and along the adjoining embankment by large horn speakers which produced a most interesting echo effect from the surrounding hills which totally confused the Speaker.

Fortunately this persuaded him he could not really compete. By the way his speech was progressing and the growing unrest of the crowd, this was probably a blessing and may even have saved him from physical injury.

The other speakers passed through with little to note until the High Sheriff took his turn. Never a man to mince his words, he praised highly all those who had transformed the station and village for the event before settling in to lambast British Rail, the Government and anyone else involved for their lack of perception of and funding for the possibilities of the area. *"This is an area of outstanding natural beauty which should be enjoyed by all!"*, he boomed, to the yells and applause of the crowd.

"If it wasn't for the work of our voluntary enthusiasts, this line would have closed years ago and yet here we are today, celebrating the fact that their perseverance has kept it operating, sometimes even at a profit, despite government's attempts to close it. Where would we be without it? How would the farmers of Castledale get their produce to market or obtain supplies during the bad weather? We know the Government won't fund a new road down the valley and yet those living in the further

settlements can so easily be cut off by snow or flood."
The crowd were going wild, this was the kind of talk they liked to hear.

The faces of the other dignitaries were a picture. The man from British Rail looked very pale as he sat with his head bowed, whilst the local MP was almost purple in the face and was chattering and gesticulating wildly to his companion. The press, who were surprisingly well represented, were delighted at the thoughts of headline possibilities and their cameras flashed incessantly.

At precisely 12 o'clock the train pulled into the station. Its smoke had been visible for some time along the line where it had been waiting by the old signal box but now it's full beauty was revealed. It was headed by an 0-6-0 tender locomotive resplendent in a fresh coat of Midland red paint with buffer beams and chimney cap in glossy black and steam couplings picked out in pristine white. The steel connecting rods and handrails shone like burnished silver, even the coal piled high in the tender sparkled. It could well have been this engine's first day at work!

Behind the engine came three open coaches, four of the small enclosed carriages which used to be so familiar on rural trains and a guards van. The whole assembly was so perfectly reminiscent of Percy's early days on the railway that he felt a tear of joy forming in the corner of his eye. On the front of the engine was fixed a board saying 'Midland Railway: Brassford - Castledale: 1894 - 1994' and this was surmounted by a bouquet of flowers. As it hissed to a stop between the stage and the far platform the press descended in a flurry of activity, cameras clicking and one of the television news crews pushed forward to try to obtain interviews with the dignitaries.

For a few minutes it seemed the stage was in danger of collapse but order was soon restored and the dignitaries quickly sought refuge in the third of the open coaches. The band were directed into the first two coaches which, on closer inspection turned out to be converted coal trucks.

These had been scrubbed clean and painted overall and had been fitted with chairs all facing backwards and fixed music stands. Someone had obviously done his homework!

By the time the band and dignitaries were settled, the carriages behind had filled with the enthusiasts who had paid a substantial sum for the privilege of travelling on this historic journey and it was time to leave. The band struck up with a rousing march which was almost instantly drowned by the train whistle which started blowing continuously as the train pulled away from the station. *"Well, that's a good start,"* thought Percy, struggling to keep his eyes fixed on the music as the train bumped over the uneven track, *"I hope the driver's not going to carry on like that all the way or we may as well not bother playing."*

The station had only just disappeared around a bend in the line when the train slowed almost to a standstill to allow a group of enthusiasts to take photographs from the top of an embankment. This process of starting and stopping was continued all the way to the next station at Midford where they were greeted by another heaving crowd. Each time the train slowed, the driver blasted his whistle, wreathing the engine and coaches in moist, humid, clinging steam.

As they pulled into Midford and squealed to a stop, the local band, who were assembled on the platform with more local worthies, launched into a slightly untuneful rendering of 'For he's a jolly good fellow'. Midford Band was another old established band but had fallen by the wayside for some years and had only been re-formed some five years ago. They had acquired sponsorship from the owners of a local quarry and wore blue uniforms with the company logo on the pockets. This, they felt, gave them an advantage over Brassford Band which they liked to air at every opportunity.

Unfortunately, their standard of music did not match their splendid attire and, on this occasion their ragged start gave Brassford a source of much mirth. Midford had been annoyed not to be given the honour of playing on the train as much of the line passed through land now owned by their sponsor and this anger now seemed to be appearing in their playing as, to the glee of the Brassford players, more and more wrong notes began to creep into their performance until they abandoned the second number altogether about half way through and sat scowling at the train whilst the Managing Director of the quarry tried to salvage the situation by an impromptu speech through a megaphone which had been produced from somewhere.

After about five minutes the train resumed its journey with more whistling and jolting and the music was again Brassfords.

Just down the line from Midford was the one real engineering feat on the line. The line of hills which bordered the right side of the valley suddenly veered to the left and blocked the railway's path along the river side.

At this point the valley formed a gorge with steep cliffs to the river and it had been necessary to form a tunnel through the hill to reach the head of the valley. This task had been undertaken by a team of about fifty Irish navvies and had been completed in record time. The feat was all the more impressive as the rock from which the hill was formed was the local limestone and was both porous and friable, making the possibility of rock falls all the more likely. Indeed, several men had lost their lives in the construction of the tunnel and a memorial to them stands at the tunnel mouth.

As the train entered the tunnel, the band were playing a selection of modern dance tunes. No sooner had they begun to consider how much better the music sounded in the resonant vault of the tunnel than the fatal flaw in the arrangements became evident. It started to get dark! They tried in vain to struggle on, playing half from memory and half by the light of the sparks from the engine's funnel but soon gave up and settled back in the gloom. By this time they were also experiencing that other joy of early travel as, sitting as they were in their open coach, they were enveloped in wreaths of choking smoke and ash from the locomotive.

The distant glimmer of daylight at the far end of the tunnel could not come soon enough and by the time they reached it everyone was coughing and covered in black smuts. Percy looked down at his jacket and shirt which had started out so pristine and at his bass on which the shine had been replaced with a dull oily film and shook his head. Perhaps the days of steam should remain only a fond memory after all!

They had acquired sponsorship from the owners of a local quarry and wore blue uniforms with the company logo on the pockets. This, they felt, gave them an advantage over Brassford Band which they liked to air at every opportunity. Unfortunately, their standard of music did not match their splendid attire and, on this occasion their ragged start gave Brassford a source of much mirth.

Midford had been annoyed not to be given the honour of playing on the train as much of the line passed through land now owned by their sponsor and this anger now seemed to be appearing in their playing as, to the glee of the Brassford players, more and more wrong notes began to creep into their performance until they abandoned the second number altogether about half way through and sat scowling at the train whilst the Managing Director of the quarry tried to salvage the situation by an impromptu speech through a megaphone which had been produced from somewhere.

After about five minutes the train resumed its journey with more whistling and jolting and the music was again Brassfords.

Just down the line from Midford was the one real engineering feat on the line. The line of hills which bordered the right side of the valley suddenly veered to the left and blocked the railway's path along the river side. At this point the valley formed a gorge with steep cliffs to the river and it had been necessary to form a tunnel through the hill to reach the head of the valley.

This task had been undertaken by a team of about fifty Irish navvies and had been completed in record time. The feat was all the more impressive as the rock from which the hill was formed was the local limestone and was both porous and friable, making the possibility of rock falls all the more likely. Indeed, several men had lost their lives in the construction of the tunnel and a memorial to them stands at the tunnel mouth. As the train entered the tunnel, the band were playing a selection of modern dance tunes.

No sooner had they begun to consider how much better the music sounded in the resonant vault of the tunnel than the fatal flaw in the arrangements became evident. It started to get dark! They tried in vain to struggle on, playing half from memory and half by the light of the sparks from the engine's funnel but soon gave up and settled back in the gloom.

By this time they were also experiencing that other joy of early travel as, sitting as they were in their open coach, they were enveloped in wreaths of choking smoke and ash from the locomotive.

The distant glimmer of daylight at the far end of the tunnel could not come soon enough and by the time they reached it everyone was coughing and covered in black smuts. Percy looked down at his jacket and shirt which had started out so pristine and at his bass on which the shine had been replaced with a dull oily film and shook his head. Perhaps the days of steam should remain only a fond memory after all!

Getting the Bird

One of the delights of playing with a village band rather than a city band is the type of people you meet. This is not to decry either country or city folk for both have their good points but, despite the regular invasions from the city, the northern countryman still retains that simplicity of outlook so beloved of music hall comedians over the years. The problems faced by country folk are generally down to earth and unique and, even when the person in question commutes and works in the city, the qualities needed to cope with these and the accompanying wry sense of humour persist.

This was the case when, calamity of calamities, the drummer's septic tank ceased to function. The principle of a septic tank is that it contains a large resident colony of friendly bacteria who happily munch away at any effluent and waste pumped their way. In this case, after years of faithful service, they had all up and died and the unsavoury waste was doing its best to fight its way out of the tank.

Rapidly, arrangements were made for the tank to be pumped out and cleaned, a costly affair which strikes at the heart of any countryman, and particularly that of Bill Jackson. Bill has the appearance and demeanour of the archetypal country farmer although his family has not actually farmed for several generations. Ruddy of face and heavily built he can generally be seen when in the village, dressed in old heavy tweeds and large leather boots and a soft tweed hat pushed back on his head.

His speech is gentle but with a very pronounced local accent, all belying the fact that during the week he is a director on the boards of several city companies and runs a very successful steel supply company. Like many of his fellow country folks, Bill chooses not to publicise the substantial wealth he undoubtedly possesses and falls naturally into the guise of a country yokel.

The defunct septic tank, however, was outside Bill's normal sphere of operations but nevertheless he was determined that he would deal with the problem himself and not squander any more of his hard won money on the task than was absolutely necessary.

Enquiries in the usual starting place of the public bar of the Millers' Arms soon suggested that a replacement family of bacteria to occupy his now vacant septic tank may be found at Gillings hardware store in the nearby market town of Wenlock - in - the - Water. It was a full day's outing to Wenlock by bus, Bill hated driving his car as he was convinced that no farmer had full control of his tractor and would therefore inevitably run into him, and it was not until late evening that he reappeared at the Millers' Arms. His return had been eagerly awaited by the clientele.

"Did you get your bugs then?" he was asked almost before he had got through the door.

"Nay lad," replied Bill *"if they think I'm paying forty quid for a bucket of bugs they can think again".*

"Forty quid, that's a bit steep isn't it?" sympathised one of the Brook brothers, *"How do they justify that kind of a price for some old bugs?"*

"I suppose it's the cost of training 'em" suggested Dick Harding.

"No, it's for choosing the ones with no sense of smell!" shouted Mandy from the pool table.

"What will you do then?" asked the barmaid.

"Well, it's funny but, on the bus home, I was talking to an old chap who reckoned that if I throw a dead hen or lamb in, then that'll do the trick".

"Oh! have a word with Joe from t'Top Farm then" chipped in the landlord *"I heard him telling Fran that one of his cockerels has just committed suicide."*

So, a visit to the adjoining games room produced a fascinating tale of a lovelorn cockerel which had been found dead in a water trough below its favourite perch, quite obviously having cast itself in in a fit of jilted depression. Several drinks later, a promise was elicited that the dead bird would be delivered to Bill on the following day for consignment into a worthy grave.

Unfortunately, Joe's memory had deteriorated with age and the effects of alcohol and it was almost a week before the constant nightly reminders eased their way into his brain and he remembered to pick up the cockerel. It was Sunday and the bar was, as usual, full of city types with their girlfriends. Band practice had just finished and there was a great deal of laughter and animated conversation when Joe entered with a rather tatty carrier bag and pushed his way to the bar.

"Has tha' seen Bill yet" he said *"only I've got him that there cockerel."*

With this, he hoisted the carrier skywards to emphasise his point and, as he did so, the rather sorry and bedraggled looking head of the bird fell through a hole in the bag bottom, swinging like a pendulum on the end of a scrawny neck which was rapidly trying to relieve itself of all its feathers. The room instantly fell silent and a clear path opened towards the tables around which the band were gathered. Seeing Bill, Joe waved and sidled across, dumping the carrier unceremoniously on the table and so causing the unfortunate bird to head-butt a glass, the contents of which cascaded over the floor.

All eyes were focused on Bill as he thanked Joe, wincing a little as, reaching over the table to shake hands, the perfume of the long dead bird reached his nostrils. Looking back at the band, Bill took his cue and excused himself, retreating with his prize to re-fertilise his waste disposal system. The next time the band met, Bill was all smiles. The cockerel had indeed 'done the trick' and his septic tank was again fully functional - and at no cost to its owner!

Playing for the Queen

The fact that the country pubs nowadays attract the Hooray Henry types from the cities provides the locals with a constant weekly source of amusement. One instance of this occurred earlier this year when the village galas were in full swing. Brassford Band had been playing for the annual May Queen festivities at a nearby village and had enjoyed themselves enormously.

The weather had been almost perfect and the crowds had been out in force. A fairground had kept the attention of most of the youngsters away from causing mischief, the parade went off without a hitch and the May Queen looked a picture. As was the custom, the band adjourned afterwards to the Millers' Arms in Brassford to discuss the days events and 'replenish the spit'.

The Millers' Arms is a quaint 'olde worlde' pub which was converted out of the old livery stables. It stands just back from the main street and has a large car park behind it in what was originally part of the church fields.

Being Sunday, the pub had acquired it's usual complement of 'townies' in their sports cars and tweed jackets, who were competing with each other to appear sophisticated and appear relaxed in the unfamiliar surroundings. Inevitably, one of them decided that he should demonstrate to his female companion that he was 'one of the boys' and, having listened to the band's conversations for some time and figured out who they were, asked the inevitable question of where they had been performing.

"Why, we've been playing for the Queen" replied Des, the Flugel horn player with a proud look.

By coincidence, there had been a visit to a neighbouring town by one of the Royal Family that day and our town friend must have half heard the mornings news.

"Well, by Jove," he exclaimed loudly, *"we are in the presence of celebrities, these chaps have spent their day entertaining our monarch."*

The noise in the bar subsided noticeably and eyes began to move towards the group.

"Did the Queen speak to you?"
asked our garrulous friend.

"Speak to us, why she took tea with us - and her attendants".

"By Jove," our friend was obviously at a loss for any better exclamation, *"I didn't know she ate with just anyone."*

"Oh, yes," a wry smile just began to creep into the corners of Des' normally deadpan mouth, *"she likes being with us country folk, she knows where she stands with us."*

"Well I'm blowed!, I never knew that but then I suppose they can't show that on the television".

"No son, they wouldn't dare let on half of what our Queen gets up to on a Sunday afternoon."

By now all the regulars in the pub were revelling in the amusement of this cross talk whilst the townies were either looking bemused or were trying their best to become inconspicuous.

At this point, Jill, one of the barmaids couldn't contain herself any longer, *"What was she wearing"* she asked, trying to maintain her best innocent expression.

"Oh, I think it was their Mary's old wedding dress, - you know, the one she bought for that posh feller that jilted her."

"Er, er, just which Queen are we talking about," stammered our city friend, the penny had obviously

dropped at last and a rosy glow of embarrassment was just beginning to tinge his cheeks.

"Why, the Haston May Queen of course, it was their Well Dressing today, which Queen did you think we were talking about?"

Grave Consequences

Every amateur organisation suffers from one major inconvenience, the need for many of its members to work for a living. This fundamental imposition often gets in the way of the serious business of enjoying oneself, particularly where shift work or unusual hours are concerned. In the case of bands, choirs, drama groups and the like the effects are felt more strongly than in most organisations as their primary vehicle of expression is the arrangement of public performances.

Unusual occupations seem to attract odd hours and at the same time spawn a type of person who is decidedly extrovert and ideally suited to the more exposed positions in a performing group - those solo spots from which the average '9 to 5 man' will shy away with an enthusiasm unknown in his daily grind. Judson Stonegrave was the eccentric extrovert's representative in the Brassford Band.

Not a very imposing person he hid his 5 ft. 8 in. frame in a hunched stoop and tried unsuccessfully to mask his lack of physique by wearing jackets several sizes too large.

These were almost always of a dark grey colour with that greasy sheen so characteristic of the 'Italian designer suits' found only at the more exclusive discount warehouses and sported shoulder pads of a size which ensured that, in speaking to him face to face, you couldn't avoid staring at the large damp stains spreading through the armpits of his unironed, heavy cotton shirts and darkening still further the sides of his jacket. On his feet he wore brown suede shoes which he swore were his only pair and which caused untold conflicts with the band's director who was a stickler for the correct uniform black shoes on public performances.

On one notable occasion, Jud had performed in black stockings with his big toes poking out after the director had refused to let him on stage in his brown suedes. Having said all this, Jud was a fine musician with a natural talent for the soprano cornet he played.

This is an extremely exposed position demanding the highest standards of musicianship as, being the highest toned instrument and having its own solo tunes singing out over the rest of the band, it is the one position which cannot fail to be identified by even the most unmusical of listeners. Judson excelled.

His clear bright notes always sailed forth over the melody in exactly the right places and gave to the overall sound that clear ringing quality which is normally the hallmark of only the best of bands. Having Jud playing at concerts gave confidence to the lesser players in the ensemble and masked or diverted attention away from the errors of some of its younger members.

However, Jud did have a rather unusual calling. He was employed as a 'junior partner' in his father's village joinery business and spent most of his days repairing old furniture, farm carts and household woodwork.

As with his music making, his craftsmanship was first rate and his skills were in particular demand over a wide area of the countryside. It was always he who was summoned to the local manor house to attend to any breakage or damage and this was always done by a personal visit from the butler.... *"His Lordship requests that you .... "*. Whilst in this employment, he was almost his own boss and he could generally manage the demands upon his time so as to give ample opportunity for band business, but the firm was also, in line with common practice, the local undertakers and, human nature being what it is, people always seem to die at the most inopportune times. So it was on the 25th. June.

The band had agreed to play a very important concert at a civic occasion in Bracclesfield, the nearest city - some 30 miles distant, on the Saturday afternoon. This honour had been bestowed on them as one of the leading city councillors had been particularly impressed by their last Christmas concert which he had attended at the 'Crown and Sparrow' (The band were hoping he had actually been impressed with their music and not just with Brassford Bottom, the local beer of which he had copiously partaken throughout the evening) and, in any case, their usual local band were away at a contest on the day in question. The concert was to begin at 4:00 pm, the funeral of Ruth Jones was scheduled for 1:30 pm with tea afterwards at Copsebottom Farm.

Normally, Jud would have left this kind of job to their hired help with his father supervising but, over the years, the Jones' had been one of the business' best customers and, besides, Jud was currently courting their eldest daughter, Ann. Consequently, Jud felt duty bound to supervise the arrangements personally. He had worked out that, if the funeral service and interment went to schedule, he should be able to leave at about 2:45 with just enough time to get to the concert venue. It would be cutting it a bit fine but with luck there would be speeches first which would give a little leeway. Just as a precaution, Jud even had a word with the vicar to elicit his agreement to being on hand early so that there would be no delay.

At first the funeral went well, the cortege arrived at the farm to pick up the relatives at one o'clock and was at the church by 1:20. So far, so good. However, Jud had reckoned without Ruth's popularity and the eulogy seemed to take an age. During her later years she had been the mainstay of the local W.I. and several other organisations within the village and the vicar felt duty bound to remind the assembled congregation of all her good works individually. By the time she was safely buried in the far corner of the graveyard it was already 3 p.m. If Jud was to be on stage in Bracclesfield at 4 o'clock he would have to get his skates on!

He had intended returning to the workshop with the hearse, changing into uniform there and using his own car for the onward journey, but to do this would take him some 5 miles out of his way and delay him far too long. So, without another thought, he set off immediately for Bracclesfield. Fortunately, he already had his cornet with him as the family had requested that he play 'the Last Post' over Ruth's grave. As regards his dress, Jud, upon due consideration, decided that in the circumstances, his old black funeral suit was as near as dammit to the band's blue and black uniform. However, even now, things didn't go smoothly and, ten minutes later, he was sitting fuming in a queue of cars at roadworks. As he sat there fretting he was undecided as to which would be his biggest problem - letting down the band by being late or facing Ann's wrath when he returned for not appearing at the funeral tea.

By the time he had passed the roadworks the decision was made and, putting his foot hard down on the accelerator, he fairly flew towards Bracclesfield. The old hearse had never gone so fast. On one section of dual carriageway it had actually touched 80 miles an hour and he was passing every other vehicle as though they were standing still. As he pulled into the car park of the concert hall, he could hear clapping from within and could hear the opening speeches.

He was met at the door by the band secretary who fairly pushed him up the stairs and onto the stage to land clumsily in his seat just as the curtains began to pull back. Fortunately his music had already been placed on his stand by one of the second cornet players and he launched into the first number with gusto, trying to appear calm and composed as the rest of the band. Only when he felt the conductor's eyes began to bite into his old black suit and his muddy brown suede shoes did he realise that he wasn't only going to have Ann to do some explaining to!

It was a week later before the second blow struck. A letter landed on the mat the following Tuesday morning bearing his address in heavy purple ink. He had seen the same handwriting before and, whilst he couldn't recall where, it gave him a premonition of doom. Falteringly, he opened the envelope and removed the single sheet of thick white paper. In the same purple hand it began....

'Dear Mr. Stonegrave,

It has been brought to the attention of the Undertakers' Federation the on 25th. June you did drive your hearse in an offensive and reckless manner between Brassford and Bracclesfield so as to bring the undertaking profession into disrepute........'

He had been spotted and reported by a competitor (he later found out who was responsible and delighted in exacting a suitable revenge) and was now called upon to face a disciplinary board to explain his actions.

Oh well, he had successfully fended off the anger of both the conductor and Ann the previous week, surely this could be no worse!

The Band Ghost

Sometimes things happen for which there is no apparent explanation. Circumstances come together in the most unusual and worrying way making you wish you had never become involved in the first place....

It all began when, out of the blue, the band were asked to play at a pie and pea supper at a hotel well out into the countryside. At first the band had been reluctant to accept the engagement as it would be difficult to arrange transport for some of the older members and some of the younger ones were in the middle of school exams. However, the fee offered was much higher than usual and as the band were desperately fund raising for uniforms for three new members it was decided to make the effort.

It was late autumn and the sun was already disappearing below the horizon as the players began to arrive.

Rain had been falling in a drizzle all afternoon and the road's covering of damp leaves deadened the sound of the cars' wheels as they coasted down the hill and into the car park. Behind the hotel, sheep grazed silently in the field as the low clouds blew gently across, periodically hiding them from view. An air of quiet stillness covered everything eerily. Inside the hotel the band were directed to a cleared area at one end of a long panelled dining room.

At one side a small bar spread a shaft of light across the room revealing an assortment of old wooden dining tables and chairs arranged haphazardly around the room. A pile of plastic chairs provided seating for the players and, as these were being set out in the usual double horseshoe with the drum kit behind to the right and the timpani to the rear left, the conductor went in search of a light switch which might give enough light to see the music.

The guests hadn't yet arrived and, whilst waiters in crumpled grey suits finished setting the tables, the band sorted their music and played a couple of pieces to warm up.

The booking had been made for 7:30 p.m. but at 7:45 no one had yet arrived. This was leading to some consternation and the conductor was just setting off on a search for the hotel manager when a trickle of guests began to arrive.

Once started, the concert seemed to go well and, even though only half the tables were occupied, a selection of wartime songs brought a rousing chorus from the older members which seemed to bring them to life. During the interval, whilst the main course was being served, the band resorted to the downstairs bar where a snack had been laid on and drinks began to flow freely amidst lively conversation. There were already several people in the bar, a family group in earnest discussion about their children's exams, a courting couple trying to merge into one of the darker corners and several older people sitting at the bar. One of these stood out from the rest. He was obviously very old with pure white hair and a full white beard devoid of even the slightest darker fleck to give away his original hair colour. His suit was clean and neat, a rough russet farmer's tweed which covered an ironed, off white, linen shirt with thin blue vertical stripes and a separate collar. His blue tie was held in place by a small gold pin. Overall he was just too smart and of too straight a bearing to be associated with the rest of the men at the bar.

As the band seated themselves at a group of tables reserved for their use, the man in the tweed suit moved from the bar and sat on a side seat close to the centre of the group. It wasn't long before he had engaged some of the younger members in conversation. As the older members joined in also it transpired that he, John, had been a member of the band in the 1930's and had, for many years played trombone until a change of job after the war had forced him to move away. Now he had returned to, as he put it, *"while away his final years in the place he loved best"*.

He had booked a meal in the hotel on the spur of the moment to ease a bout of depression and had not known about the band's performance, but now this had brought memories flooding back and he was anxious to share them with the present members. The fact that he was now missing the main course of the meal seemed irrelevant to him as he recounted anecdote after anecdote about the past glories of the band.

Most of the band found this fascinating - yes there had originally been a 'silver prize' which had been won in competition by the band on three consecutive occasions so giving them the right to add the wording to their name - and it was with some regret that they returned to the dining room for the second half of the concert. However, they couldn't let John go without inviting him to a rehearsal and promising that a spare trombone would be there for him to play.

Many of the older and more sceptical members thought that this was the last they would see of old John but, sure enough, John was waiting at the door as they arrived for rehearsal on Sunday evening. Despite the fact that he was now well into his eighties, John was full of energy and enthusiasm and, seated amongst the trombone section, he took a pair of gold rimmed half glasses from his inside pocket and scanned the music intently.

The first couple of pieces were a struggle for him, he had apparently not played for a number of years, and the music was quite modern and new to him, however, when the next piece was announced as 'Colonel Bogey' his eyes sparkled and, instrument held high, he played most of his part from memory as though he had never been away from a band.

For the next two years he never missed a rehearsal and became a kind of second grandfather to the younger players, encouraging and helping them in their music making and listening patiently to all their little stories and problems. Obviously, age slowed John's movements down a little and he preferred to play the slower music and sometimes sat out the faster and more complicated pieces. His favourite tune was 'Amazing Grace' and he would often ask if this could be played to finish the practice. However, for some reason, John would always play one note wrong, playing a B natural instead of a B flat in the nineteenth bar. Normally the error was ignored but occasionally someone would point it out to him afterwards and he would just shrug his shoulders and say, *"Yes, I know, but I was sure I'd blown the right one that time."*

Then John was taken ill and died. The band insisted on marching in front of the hearse and played 'Amazing Grace' at the graveside while most of the village stood around singing the words in a murmur as if to themselves. John had certainly made himself popular during the short time he had been back in the village.

For many months rehearsals were not the same joyful affairs as usual and the music for 'Amazing Grace' was returned to the filing cabinet as no one could bring themselves to play it. However, early the following year, a letter arrived from the local Member of Parliament asking the band to play at a society wedding and to be sure to include 'Amazing Grace' as part of the programme as it was the particular favourite of the bride's mother.

After a great deal of soul searching and spirited discussion in the band it was decided that the piece would have to return to the repertoire at some time and this might as well be the time. After all, John had been buried for almost a year and they had decided at the outset that they would play it on the anniversary of his death which would be in the week preceding the wedding and so, at the next rehearsal, the music was again on the stands.

As they played the first bars, a wave of emotions passed over almost every member and the sound wavered a little over the quiet opening section. The tone steadied as the tune built in volume but, as they reached the twentieth bar playing suddenly ceased and players looked round at each other questioningly. The section was repeated but each time the band broke off at the twentieth bar. The first time may have been imagination but not now, there was definitely a B natural being played by someone in the nineteenth bar! Thinking it a practical joke in poor taste, each player was quizzed and made to play the section individually but to no avail.

Then the band was made to play the section over and over without different players, each time the B natural appeared. After the same situation occurring at each practice for three weeks the band began to joke about John's ghost still playing with them but it was really all quite disconcerting and the piece was approached with some trepidation for the remaining four weeks leading up to the remembrance service which was to be held for John in the local Methodist church.

During the service the B natural made its appearance again and a brief announcement was made to try to explain its presence although this was hardly necessary as the story had circulated around the village and surrounding area weeks before and many of the locals would have been disappointed had it not been there. Strangely, at the wedding the following week, the tune came over perfectly and this caused as much surprise amongst the players as had the wrong note before.

To this day the band still plays 'Amazing Grace', always note perfect but never without a memory of old John and his ghost's assistance!

The Seeing Eye

One of the main problems which besets a small local band is moving all their equipment around the countryside for engagements. Over the years Brassford have used almost every mode of transport from horse drawn farm wagon to train. At one time it was a common sight to see the village postman cycling along to a rehearsal or a concert with his tuba strapped to his back and Bill Turpin had made a special bracket to hold his bass drum like a spare wheel on the side of his dog cart.

Inevitably, one of the busiest times for the band was always the few weeks before Christmas when the sound of a traditional brass band could lull even the most hardened cynic into a warm haze of conviviality. Also, of course, this was also the worst time of year for bad weather with frosts and chilling mists. So it was on the day of the annual Oddfellows carol concert at Hatherton.

The day had started with a flurry of snow which turned into a steady drizzle for most of the morning. The concert was to be at 2:00 p.m. in the Village Hall and, as it was a fair distance from Brassford and the transport of the larger instruments would otherwise be a problem, it had been decided to accept the offer of the free use of Toby Wilson's old coach 'Betsy'. This was a vintage vehicle in every sense of the word. Built in about 1939 it had seen service as the local bus for 30 years until even the local vehicle examiner could turn a blind eye no longer. The it had become home to Jim Green's three goats for ten years after which it was acquired in exchange for an old lawn mower by Will Garlick who 'did it up a bit' and lived in it on waste land by the railway embankment until he died last year. Now it had been taken in hand by Toby who was in the process of 'restoring it to its former glory'.

Inevitably this work was quite slow and, whilst the mechanics of the vehicle had been repaired to such an extent that it could be just considered roadworthy, the remainder of the vehicle left a lot to be desired. It had no fixed seats but was equipped with a three piece suite and a couple of old dining chairs, the bodywork was rusted to resemble lace and was largely held together by the remains of the faded blue and white paintwork. Through the destination board windows moth caterpillars could be seen devouring the last remains of the cloth destination blinds.

However, Toby was convinced that the bus would hold together long enough for the journey and was anxious to help and so the band agreed so long as they could set off in plenty of time 'just in case'. Originally it was intended to put all the instruments in the baggage lockers under the bus but when it was realised that none of these had floors in them a rethink became necessary. There would not be sufficient room in the bus for both the band and their instruments and, in any case no one was prepared to risk the bus floor with all that weight. A committee meeting was called. After much deliberation and argument a plan of action was formulated and various members were dispatched to acquire the necessary accessories. Within half an hour people were swarming all over the bus and a roof rack made from ladders and scaffolding was beginning to take shape which gave all the appearance of being twice as strong as the bus itself. Onto this was loaded the instruments and, with the rest of the band inside, the bus set off on its precarious journey.

To the amazement of all, the journey there was without further incident and the band arrived so early that, surprisingly, they had to pass away some time in the 'Bulls Mouth'. This relieved all tensions so that, by the time of the carol concert, everyone was in such a good mood that the concert turned out a great success. However, when everything was packed away and the band emerged from the hall, their spirits fell with a bump.

While they had been enjoying themselves, darkness had fallen and worse still fog had appeared. You couldn't see more than ten feet in front of you and the fog seemed to cling to everything. Toby, however, was as effusive as ever and was enthusiastically hoisting the instruments up onto the roof of the bus and chivvying everyone along.

*"Come on, we'll not be back before
the chip shop shuts!"*

The usually ebullient band were unusually quiet.

*"How on earth are we going to find our way home
in this fog"* asked Jim with a worried frown.

"Oh! don't worry" said Toby *"we'll manage,
just leave everything to me and good old
Betsy. We'll get you home alright"*.

No one was really convinced. Indeed, as they left the car park it was difficult to determine whether they had actually turned onto the road or were just heading off across the fields. The headlights, such as they were, gave out only a dim glow which was reflected back onto the oil smeared windscreen by the swirling fog making the view forward almost non-existent. Toby, however, did not seem unduly bothered and was humming the last tune of the concert gaily to himself as the bus bowled along at a steady twenty miles an hour.

Most of the band were petrified. *"For goodness
sake slow down"* urged Janet from the back ,*"it's
my birthday next week and I've already baked a
cake, it wouldn't look right at a funeral tea!"*.

"Stop worrying," chided Toby *"I know what I'm doing.
Unless someone comes the other way, which I doubt
in this weather, we are OK. for at least ten miles."*

"But how the heck do you know where we are?"

"Aha! that's one of our little secrets, isn't it Betsy?"

But the further along they travelled, the more fretful became the band. Noses were pressed to every window, straining to catch even a glimpse of a hedgerow through the all-pervading gloom.

"What on earth has that man got - Radar?" asked Jack of no one in particular, *"he doesn't even seem to be looking at the road. I'm going to try to find out his secret, the military would probably pay highly for a secret weapon like him!"*

All the rest of the band had, by now, gravitated to the back of the bus, reasoning that if they were going to run into something, they would be in the safest place.

Gingerly making his way up the rocking bus, Jack clutched onto the back of Toby's seat. *"Are you sure you know where you are going?"* he whispered breathlessly only too aware of the eerie yellow glow in the windscreen.

"Of course," laughed Toby *"do you think I'm a fool? You all thought old Betsy is just a rusty wreck but age and experience count for a lot in weather like this. See that hole in the floor under the pedals, well, all I need to do is keep that over the white line in the middle of the road and we're OK. till we get to Hatherton cross roads, then we turn left and it's follow the line again right into Brassford. We should be in time for a bag of chips before Fanny's closes."*

61

"We'll need it, you wily old bird, and something to wash 'em down with."

"I'm sure that can be arranged. Now will you go and sit down again and let me concentrate?"

Economic Living

Dove cottage in Brassford is one of the oldest and prettiest dwellings in the village and, set within low stone walls enclosing a small tidy garden full of hollyhocks, dog daisies, lupins, sweet williams and other such traditional fragrant flowers, attracts almost as many inquisitive and appreciative tourists and visitors as its flowers do bees. Standing on the main road just across from the Post Office and the Village Hall, it is at the very focus of the village and thus could only logically be inhabited by a gregarious and extrovert person, well able to accept the attention which living there inevitably receives.

True to type, this inhabitant had for many years been Effie Wallace, a spinster who had been born 73 years ago within sight of the cottage and who had served the village all her life as school teacher, headmistress, choir mistress and organiser of the local Women's Institute. In her 'spare' time over the last fifty years she had played with the band where she played a mean tenor horn - an instrument which itself sneaks up on the music with extrovert passages or cheekily doubles the cornet's tune in a lower register.

Recently, however, bronchitis and badly fitting false teeth had robbed her of the ability to meet the band's standards and so she had voluntarily dropped out to play a lesser role in the background. Despite the obvious restrictions on active participation, her interest in the band had never waned and many of the tasks which she now undertook were ones which she had created herself to maintain this interest. Just such a task was the 'keeping of seats' in the Fox and Duck after rehearsals on a Sunday evening.

The 'L - shaped' pub, whilst quite old, had been remodelled to brewery standards and was now divided into a number of 'bays' by mock Tudor woodwork and beams, each of which was populated by several small tables and stools comfortably upholstered in fake leather. From about 7:30 pm each Sunday, Effie could be found sitting in the very centre of the largest of these bays, fending off any stray drinker with designs on a comfortable seat until the band arrived for their post rehearsal relaxation just after 9 o'clock. None of the regulars would tangle with Effie's sharp tongue and chose instead to respect the efficiency with which she carried out her self imposed duty.

Visitors, of course, were not to know, and many learnt to their cost Effie's perception of the needs and privileges earned by the band over their years of dedication, so much so that quite often a quiet word or a free drink was required from the landlord or the band's director later in the evening to smooth the visitor's ruffled feathers. However, no one would think of saying anything to Effie as she was too well liked to be upset.

As time passed and Effie's health waned, she spent more and more time in the pub where she would sit in a corner most evenings behind a half finished glass of stout discussing the state of the world with anyone who would speak to her.

Living just across the road, Janet, the postmistress and long time co-conspirator of Effies on the tenor horn row, had fallen into the task of being Effie's 'minder'.

She would call in at Effie's house once or twice a day as business allowed just to make sure she was OK and would do her weekly shopping on a Thursday after the Post Office closed for the afternoon. She would also be the one to keep Effie in touch with band gossip and make sure that someone would be available to drive Effie to any band concerts as she would have been devastated to find that she had missed one.

One Sunday evening last November, Effie had done her usual good job and almost the whole band were comfortably seated in the busy pub. The atmosphere bubbled with laughter and jovial banter as everyone released the last of the pent up steam before descending into the doldrums of Monday morning at work. Effie had already had three halves of mild before the band arrived and, as different members of the group bought rounds which always included her, the row of empty glasses in front of her threatened to overwhelm the table.

As the band began to split up and make for home, Des, mindful that while Effie was showing no obvious signs of intoxication and was clearly still enjoying herself, the six pints or so of mild ale which she had consumed by then must have had some effect, said, *"Come on Effie, I'll walk you home."*

"You'll do no such thing, young man" came the sharp reply, *"I'm perfectly capable of getting home on my own and anyway, it's not time yet. You can get me another drink though."*

"Don't you think you've had enough now?" said Des, *"you must have had about six pints already."*

"Rubbish! Six pints indeed! I know exactly how many I've had and that's three small glasses all evening."

"Three small glasses, but what about all these empties lined up on the table?"

"Oh, I don't know about them, they're not relevant. You can only count the drinks you pay for yourself!"

Obviously not in a winning position, Des realised that his pleas would have no effect upon the strong will of Effie and so he left her sitting alone in the now emptying pub. On his way home he called in at Janet's just to let her know how he had had to leave Effie and with a suggestion that a visit in the morning might not go amiss. But it didn't get that far.

After the band left, Effie was befriended by a couple of tourists who were staying in the pub and together they spent a happy and animated couple of hours exchanging stories and reminiscences. By about 1:30, however, with none of the participants showing signs of running out of material, the landlord finally decided enough was enough and that he would dearly like to close up and fall into the arms of Morpheus.

Unfortunately, Effie had other ideas and, with help from her surfeit of alcohol, started to become belligerent. Hadn't she been his best customer of the evening? Hadn't she made sure that the band had swelled his till until it almost burst? She would go when she was ready and not before!

Eventually, it all became too much for the poor landlord and he had to send for reinforcements - Janet! Dragged from her sweet slumbers and dressed only in an old raincoat and wellingtons over her nighty, she was not in the best of moods as she squared up to Effie and demanded that she stop making such a fuss and allow her to make sure she got home safely.

"Oh well, I suppose I shall have to if you're all going to gang up on me," said Effie, *"but I'm really not ready for bed and it will be such a waste to have to use my own electric light!"*

Christmas Carolling

Christmas must be the busiest time of year for any band. It is the time when fund-raising efforts move into top gear and for a few weeks before the festivities begin in earnest all other considerations are shelved whilst everyone is re-equipped with carol books and Christmas selections. Like many bands who play for their own amusement and the pleasure of others rather than in competition, Brassford Band must raise over £5000 each year just to keep going.

Practice facilities must be paid for, music must be bought, damaged and worn instruments must be repaired or replaced and uniforms must be kept in good order. Fortunately, Christmas provides a fine occasion for fund-raising as the stirring and well loved tunes persuade even the most miserly to part with a few pennies.

Of course, carolling can have its drawbacks which inevitably supply the necessary humour to overcome the effects of chill winds and snow falling gently down the back of one's neck. Unlike the buskers so often seen in our cities sadly churning out bedraggled versions of the same few carols with boring repetition, the tradition in the smaller villages is for the band to make its way around the village pausing every few yards to play a different tune whilst their enthusiastic supporters visit each house in turn to elicit a donation.

This is a slow process which, even in the case of a meagre village like Brassford, can take several trips to complete due to the generous nature of the inhabitants. For many, this is considered a social event and it would be considered a positive affront if the band did not pause at their gate and accept the token hospitality of a hot mince pie and glass of spirit. Obviously, it doesn't take many such stops, which of course the band feel duty bound to accept, for the whole purpose of the day's outing to be forgotten.

Surrounding villages are not immune from the band's attentions at Christmas and a visit to one of the more out of the way hamlets took on an entirely undeserved frustration. In their normal fashion, the band had been working their way from one end of the village to the other, stopping frequently to play a carol and knocking on every door that showed signs of life. It had been a cold evening, fine but frosty, and the chill was beginning to eat into everyone's bones.

The villagers here were not quite as friendly as in Brassford and no warming pies or spirits had been offered. As they neared the end of the main street it was jointly decided that after one more carol stop they would pack up and head for home. The collecting tin was by no means full and usually no house would be left without the chance of contributing but this night was just too cold for comfort. They paused outside a small cottage and played a couple of verses of Once in Royal David's City' for which the old lady living in the cottage donated fifty pence. As they turned to make their way back to the other end of the village and their cars Jack Green spotted a light on a building about fifty yards up a track just off the main street.

"Let's just do that last one up there," he suggested, *"it seems a shame to miss the last one."*

Reluctantly the others agreed and they made their way up the track as far as a gate.

"We'll play here" said Bill *"while you go and collect".*

Again the strains of 'Once in Royal.......' echoed around the valley while Jack made his way tentatively up the muddy path into the darkness. Two verses later Jack had not returned.

"Shall we play it again?"

"Yes, I suppose we'd better. Maybe he's having difficulty making anyone hear."

Another two verses bounced back from the hills. Still no sign of Jack. The band were just pondering their next step when Jack's dishevelled form re-appeared at the gate.

"I'm sure there's someone in there but I'm damned if I can make them hear." he said *"Play it again and I'll give it another go."*

So off he went again while the band played a fifth verse and then a sixth.

Again Jack appeared. *"I still can't make them hear, perhaps we'd better just forget this one."*

"Forget it be blowed," Bill spluttered *"after six verses I reckon they owe us something. I'll go this time."*

Half way into the eighth verse Bill returned, red in the face and obviously not best amused. *"Pack up,"* he yelled *"thanks to this daft lummock we've just spent the last half hour playing to a ruddy barn full of cows!"*

Occasionally, the collectors can get carried away as happened a couple of years ago. Again it was quite a cold and damp night, the band had been playing earlier in the day for an open air service around the village crib and some of the band members were quite reluctant to extend the carolling longer than necessary.

The village was, however, the home of one of the trombonists, Jim Arnthwaite and he was anxious to show off 'his' band to all his neighbours and to demonstrate to the band how generous his neighbours could be. Rather than the usual procedure of play a carol, then move on a few yards and play another, it was decided that they would play at strategic street corners and collectors would go around all the houses within range.

This village was larger than Brassford and its layout favoured this approach. Whilst the band struck up with 'O come all ye faithful', the collectors set off, including Jim. Soon his enthusiasm got the better of him and he was ranging further and further from the band at each stop. After about an hour and a half the band had had enough. For the last twenty minutes they had not seen hide nor hair of Jim but just assumed that he had stopped for a talk somewhere and would catch up in due course. It had already been decided that the band would adjourn afterwards to one of the local pubs to warm up again and assess the profitability of the evening and so they now made their way to the Red Lion close to where the cars were parked.

The collecting boxes of the other collectors revealed a total of £46, not bad for an evening's work but where was the all important box of Jim's, surely that would admirably swell the coffers. It was another half hour before Jim finally turned up, some of the band had already left for home and the rest were just about to.

"Where on earth did you get to?" he spluttered.
"Oh, we gave up about an hour ago. Where were you?"

"I was still out collecting, waiting for you to appear!"

The band was not too popular for a few days with Jim but he soon came to see the funny side of the situation when all was revealed. It transpired that in his excitement Jim had covered almost all of the village single handed and was rushing round knocking on doors and assuring the occupants that 'the band will be along in just a minute' until well after the band had retired to the warmth of the Red Lion. His collecting tin alone provided another £56 towards funds which, whilst some of it had been acquired under false pretences, gave a very welcome boost to band finances.

It would be wrong to assume from the foregoing that all the band is concerned with over Christmas is its own fund-raising; certainly this does play an important part in the series of events but is by no means the main part of them. Christmas is also a time for freely giving to others in the form of concerts, church services and visits to local old folks' homes and children's homes. There are also the traditional aspects of playing for the dedication of the crib in the village square and entertaining in the local pubs who tolerate the sometimes boisterous musicians for the rest of the year. All these events have to be fitted into the month before Christmas and around New Year.

Playing in the churches of Brassford and the surrounding villages and market towns can, in itself, be a real joy. Almost without exception these churches, from the most elaborate to the simplest, provide the kind of acoustic environment which enhances the sound of brass instruments and gives both the players and the listeners shivers down their backs.

The faces of the congregation experiencing the full force of the music in the more substantial carols and the sensitive roundness of the more delicate melodies are a joy to behold. This, of course, is not really surprising when one visits some of these same churches at other times of the year and hears the unkempt organs and squeaky harmoniums to which their congregations are usually subjected.

Epilogue

Thank you for reading this book.

A book such as this can only touch on the multitude of amusing occurrences and personalities encountered by the band during any normal year. I have tried in these pages to give a flavour of the richness and diversity of 'life at the sharp end' which is repeated time and again in bands and other such organisations throughout the country, indeed, throughout the world.

The only real way to fully experience the pleasure of incidents such as are recorded here is to become involved, not necessarily in bands but perhaps in local theatre groups, Women's Institute, or youth organisations. All offer sources of amusement and interest for those who seek them and add immeasurably to the rich tapestry of life.

Before I close, I must offer my sincere thanks to Paul Smith and the late John Howard and several other members of the South Yorkshire and North Derbyshire brass banding community whose innate ability to distil the comic elements from often seemingly mundane occurrences and whose natural skills as raconteurs have inspired the recording of a number of the stories in this book.

Without people like them the world would be a far duller place.

About the Author

Ian W. Wright has been associated with brass bands for many years playing a variety of instruments from Tenor Horn through Baritone and Euphonium to Tuba. His brass banding career began when he introduced his young son to a band, having been advised that advised it would help with his asthma – two weeks later, Ian was also sitting in the band with a shiny baritone in his hand! ("No use just sitting at the side waiting son, you might as well be learning to play" was the comment of the conductor, thrusting the instrument into rather reluctant hands).

Nearly 40 years on, Ian is still playing, though now on a tuba – the biggest and most demanding instrument in the band. Over these years, he has played with bands of all abilities from village bands to championship bands and also with wind bands and orchestras - and he has enjoyed every minute of it!

Now retired from a demanding job in local government, Ian enjoys family life and also indulging himself in his other hobbies of watchmaking, restoring scientific antiques and painting.